ZENSHO W. KOPP

NOW
is Eternity

Our true self is pure, radiating being and eternal bliss.

The key to perceiving our true essence and to leading a meaningful life lies in returning to our divine nature within our innermost depths.

In the light of pure, crystal-clear awareness you perceive your true essence, which is immortality.

Only the present moment is real. Past and future exist only in your mind, but your true essence reveals itself now-here, beyond the illusion of space and time.

All things are like a dream, a vision, petals out of nothing; chasing after them is completely pointless.

Therefore, free yourself of all illusory notions and live free and unbound in the world, without attaching to anything.

The moment the conditioned limitation of the own mind falls, the narrow consciousness of your pseudo-individuality with its perceived external world of phenomena disappears and your heart opens to the boundless love of divine being.

The Zen way to liberation does not tolerate any dependence on anything at all.

Shatter all your limitations! Liberate yourself from all your concepts and you will abide in the boundless freedom of the mind.

All phenomena are a revelation of the one reality and pervade each other completely and harmonically, without any form of hindrance.

 As soon as the self-mind has been beheld, all discrimination ceases and you awaken from your dream of a three dimensional external world of phenomena.

Where there is clear, present awareness there is also meditation. Without it, there is no true meditation.

When you endeavour in your meditation, your awareness will soon be so great that meditation will take place of its own accord.

The external world of phenomena is the game of the mind. If you take it to be real, you will be deceived by the projections in your own mind. Everything is just an illusory spectacle.

Yet behind all thinking – beyond the illusion of space and time – the radiating light of the mind, your true essence, reveals itself.

Since you as a person are a manifestation of the infinite in this changing world of finitude, the absolute necessity arises for you to realise the infinite within this finite world as your true essence.

When you immerse yourself in your inner ground and completely abandon your notion of "I" and all things, you will recognise that you are the sole-existing reality beyond birth and death.

This knowledge of your true essence is at the same time the knowledge of the fundamental reality of all that exists.

It is essential that the mind comes to rest in a natural way, free of distractions and intentions, and without any wanting on your part to force it.

Without the compulsive activity of the intellect, a state of authenticity arises and you are at rest in the directness of pure being.

The phenomena that the consciousness perceives only become shackles when there is wanting and rejecting.

Therefore, abide beyond all discrimination in the directness of Now and rest steadfastly in natural awareness of mind.

True belief is much more than just super-ficially assuming something to be true.

True belief is unswerving trust that has opened itself to divine being in the depths of the heart and can never be lost.

Crucifixion means crossing out everything that is covering your true essence. It is the crossing-out of the ego-delusion.

You yourself are the cause of all obstacles. Therefore, free yourself of your ego-notion and you will experience the boundless expanse of the mind.

It is fundamentally important that you stop the constantly fabricating mind by totally focussing your full attention on Now.

You are already in the midst of the fullness of divine being, which is constantly present. However, you can only experience it when you and your consciousness are completely present in Here and Now.

Desirelessness is the jewel that fulfils all desires. However, thinking constantly creates desires.

Let go of your self-perpetuating compulsion to constantly think, and immerse yourself in your true essence. Thus, your mind will become restful in the peace of contentedness.

Body, mind and world are only fleeting, passing phenomena that float across the eternally un- changing reality like clouds covering the moon.

This reality is the sole, true essence. It is your eternal, true self. It is pure, brightly shining consciousness, completely detached from every- thing and is absolute blissfulness.

Your true essence is unborn and undying since it is beyond birth and death.

At the moment of death, only body and world-perception die, yet not you in your true, eternal being.

All things arise through and in your own mind.

Bad thoughts give rise to hell, good thoughts give rise to paradise.

Only those who, in their spiritual striving, have reached the limits of their thinking will be able to risk the leap into the great void.

It is the leap into boundlessness – into the immeasurable original ground of divine being.

There is no individual personality, separate from the all-embracing whole, just as there is no wave that is different from the other waves on the ocean.

Everything is the one ocean, everything is the One Mind in its all-embracing wholeness.

When thoughts arise, the confusion of multiplicity arises. When thoughts cease, the multiplicity ceases and the mind abides in detached clarity.

All thought dispersion ends in the peaceful silence of the mind, since the mind ceases its occupation with the unreal.

In the deep meditation of Samadhi, the memory of body, mind and world ceases of its own accord, consciousness activity comes to a halt and your perception transforms into the wisdom-eye of transcendental knowledge.

Spiritual realisation is when everything falls away from you that is not you, and the sole remainder is that which you have been in your true essence for all eternity and will eternally be.

Through intensive, constant single-mindedness in all activities, perception and action merge into one and you transcend all obstacles.

This undivided concentration of present awareness in all activities is the great steadfastness of the mind in which you experience all things as manifestations of the one reality.

The individual mind is just a reflection, emanating from absolute consciousness. Therefore, turn your mind around, back to its original source.

Experience each moment of vibrant presence in complete awareness and you will experience all-uniting love with all beings.

The true self is the light of your mind. In this light, all things are revealed.

The light of your true self creates the perception of the external world. By letting go of dualistic thinking the entire universe will dissolve in your own heart.

The path of spiritual transformation is the practice of dissolving all duality into the experience of unity of non-discriminating clarity of mind.

When you liberate yourself from all notions of God, regardless of how holy they may be, you will reach a vibrant experience of God.

When the flow of rising thoughts suddenly ceases, you will experience that the own mind and the One Mind are a single reality.

You experience that your mind is pristine, boundless and completely free.

The ego is constantly fleeing from absolute Now because it only obtains its pseudo-existence through identification with the interwoven memories of its dead past and its desires, projected into the future.

Since you are Buddha in your true essence, the best and easiest way to Buddhahood is when, rather than seeking externally, you constantly focus your mind on itself so that it recognises its original, enlightened buddha-nature.

When in this life, you truly endeavour to constantly uphold the presence of pure aware-ness, you have the great possibility at the moment of death of experiencing enlighten-ment.

You are as much in your true self as you are at rest, and as much outside of your true self as you are in unrest.

Enlightenment is the experience of your immortality.

It is the knowledge that your true essence is unborn, unfading and is eternal bliss, for it is birthless and deathless highest reality.

Fundamental, underlying reality can only be conceived by a pure mind beyond discriminating, conceptual thinking.

It is unchanging in the midst of all change, re-mains constantly unchanging within itself and is beyond life and death.

By realising a higher perception through spiritual clarity, inner and outer become a completely transparent unity and are experienced as pure mind.

Your problems are nothing other than autonomous thinking. You can liberate yourself from them in an instant.

True seclusion is a consciousness state of inner detachment from everything, coupled with a profound experience of your true essence.

Do not seek God internally or externally, but rather be inwardly silent and allow yourself to be found by Him.

By realising crystal-clear awareness, you experience everything as an omnipresent revelation of divine reality.

This liberation from dualistic perceptions leads you to a universal, higher awareness in life and thus in death too.

When you are completely one with yourself, you are one with everything.

You experience the great peace of your true self, everywhere and at all times.

Abide constantly, everywhere and at all times in non-discriminating awareness of the present instant.

Never deviate from this, then death cannot take you by surprise.

You think you are moving in an external world of space and time but it is like when you are dreaming at night. In truth, it is only the mind that moves.

The practice of dream yoga lies in being aware of dreaming, even in the dream state, and in recognising everything as one's own projection.

You achieve fearlessness of mind when your consciousness abides ever-present in the direct moment of Now.

Simply be completely natural and relaxed. See things as they are, without projecting discriminating thoughts.

You can only find the truth and real peace in your inner true self, for within you is the divine light, which is eternal peace and endless bliss.

The more you have inwardly let go of all things, the closer you are to divine light, love and oneness with highest reality.

In the darkness of inner silence, when all thinking ceases, the divine light radiates forth as your true essence.

When your discriminating thinking abruptly ceases, your own mind reveals itself as the reality of the One Mind, piercingly bright in the boundless expanse of its own light.

Since things are sublime in their thusness, spontaneous realisation takes place at the moment of perceiving the true nature of things and your mind.

The moon, the mountains, rivers and all beings are no longer separate from one another and are experienced as One in the beginningless eternity of here and now.

If you wish to experience the reality of your true essence, you must transcend space and time and corporeality, and perceive your deathless eternity.

In this great experience of your fundamental essence, when all thoughts cease, you clearly experience that the Self-Mind is pristinely pure, unborn, immeasurably radiating and completely free.

When transcendental wisdom with its boundless light shines forth within you and illuminates both inner and outer, you perceive your original mind as your true self.

Only when it has become completely dark as night within you will the inner sun of realisation of your true essence rise.

Raise your consciousness above the illusion of space and time and establish it firmly in your innermost, divine ground.

Immerse yourself within yourself until you reach your origin. Only there will you find true peace and contentment.

The intellect, entangled in objectification, will cease its activity in deep meditation and intentionless perception. Without the entanglement of desiring, there is no concept of a goal to be achieved.

When all thoughts dissolve, clear consciousness remains that experiences itself as pure Being.

When your consciousness rests completely relaxed in crystal-clear, open awareness of mind, free of thoughts, the experience of merging with a boundless expanse takes place.

It is a spiritual state, which you live as joyful clarity, without the slightest discrimination externally or internally.

Spiritual delusion only takes place because the fixated intellect objectifies everything. However, your original mind is agelessly free and boundless vastness, in which objects have never existed.

When dualistic thinking ceases, spontaneous, present consciousness appears from within itself in natural purity and clarity.

The more you trust in divine being, the less you trust in your own dualistic intellect.

This great trust opens your mind for the action of divine grace.

If you wish to experience the pure, original state of your true essence, you must firstly purify your heart from all attachment, grasping and rejecting.

Once your heart is completely pure and clear, you will experience everywhere the original, pure state of your true essence.

Just as there is no difference between the sun and its radiation, so too are thoughts just the mind's energy and not distinct from it.

Without becoming distracted, just observe them during meditation without attaching and abide relaxed in present awareness.

Imprint

First edition 2021

Original title "Das Jetzt ist die Ewigkeit,"
published by Spirit Rainbow Verlag, Aachen, Germany 2020

Original idea and design: Verena Kopp
Image editing: Reinhard Zanella, Sandro Hölzel
Translation: John Kitching
Typesetting: Reinhard Zanella
Cover design: Michel Schmidt
Back cover photo: Axel Jung

Herstellung und Verlag:

BoD Books on Demand, Norderstedt

ISBN 9783754323366

Image Credits

Shutterstock – ViSnezh – Image nr. 337822397
www.shutterstock.com/de/g/Snezh
Designed by rawpixel.com / Freepik

Zensho W. Kopp, born 1938, is one of the most significant spiritual masters of the present and teaches a contemporary way to spiritual realisation.

The internationally renowned Zen master and author of numerous spiritual books instructs a large community of students and directs the Zen Center Tao Chan in Wiesbaden, Germany.

Tao Chan Zentrum e.V., Non-profit society, Wiesbaden

Open Zen-evening: Twice a month, the Zen Center Tao Chan in Wiesbaden organises an open Zen-evening, directed by Zen Master Zensho W. Kopp.

Information and registration: **www.tao-chan.org**
Visit our Facebook site at **www.facebook.com/zensho.w.kopp**.
A selection of the master's video talks can be found at **www.tao-chan.org/zen-master-zensho/videos.html**

Further books by Zensho W. Kopp

104 pages, 9,80 €

ISBN 9783752670554

116 pages, 9,80 €

ISBN 9783751957731

140 pages, 11,99 €

ISBN 9783751931823

or audiobook, 15,00 €

120 pages, 7,95 €

ISBN 9783842328617

or audiobook, 15,00 €

Modern ZEN-ART	136 pages	ISBN 9783907246092	23,50 €
Enlightened Dimensions of the Divine	140 pages	ISBN 9781482799422	10,50 €
The ZEN Ox-herding Pictures	212 pages	ISBN 9783753421490	9,95 €
The direct ZEN-Way to Liberation	220 pages	ISBN 9783752641158	12,50 €
True Life Through Zen	140 pages	ISBN 9783734743559	11,50 €
The Freedom of Zen	216 pages	ISBN 9783751954648	12,95 €
Words of the Awakened Mind	120 pages	ISBN 9783848241347	9,95 €

All publications by Zensho can be found and purchased here:
www.tao-chan.org/zen-master-zensho/books.html